HANNAH'S OTHER BOOKS ARE:

"Altars of remembrance"
"More altars of remembrance"
"Endless altars of remembrance"
"New Wine"
"Unworthy but accepted"

A NEW VISION: IT IS NEVER TOO LATE

HANNAH CASAREZ

WESTBOW
PRESS®
A DIVISION OF THOMAS NELSON
& ZONDERVAN

WestBow Press books may be ordered through booksellers or by contacting:

WestBow Press
A Division of Thomas Nelson & Zondervan
1663 Liberty Drive
Bloomington, IN 47403
www.westbowpress.com
844-714-3454

Scripture quotations are taken from the New King James Version®. Copyright © 1982 by Thomas Nelson. Used by permission. All rights reserved.

ISBN: 979-8-3850-0044-9 (sc)
ISBN: 979-8-3850-0045-6 (e)

Print information available on the last page.

WestBow Press rev. date: 6/6/2023

CONTENTS

NEVER LEFT OR FORSAKEN

This is my sixth book, and it looks like my God is doing something new in my life. Having been on staff with Campus Crusade for Christ forty-five years, I still have a fulltime job there. The 63 overseas trips to 27 countries have been indescribable adventures and blessings. I have shared most of them in my previous books. Because I am turning 85 on November 11 in '22, my overseas travels have been denied. I could never forget those precious times and those new believers the Lord used me for. What a joy to have a part in their lives.

My sadness was relieved by a new vision from my beloved Creator. My first book came from notes I write after my quiet times or Bible studies. Posting my impressions keeps me in touch with my Savior on a daily basis and gives me the instructions and guidance He promised in Psalms 32:8. He says, "I will instruct you and teach you in the way you should go, I will counsel you with my eye on you." This is what I dwell on and claim often.

The forty-eight years since my God saved me, have been shared in my past five books and this one, and I will continue till my God says, "all done." As of 2022, my family has grown to twenty-five great grandchildren and my first two great-great grand kids. One of my great grandsons is in the Army and stationed in Hawaii and is finishing his service time. The great grandson that is in the Navy only comes home for Christmas.

My youngest son and family are living in Kentucky, where I get to visit once a year, all others are right around me, which I love. Being also a member of "The Joy Company", which is a ministry to city schools, is a dear blessing to me. This keeps me involved with about 28-30 high school youth for Bible studies, leadership training and sorted outreach activities. They have anxiously waited to finish Jr-high and now joined us for this new semester together with the seniors.

TEACHING YOUNG PEOPLE IS SO SATISFYING.

E ven during the summer these beautiful and spiritual programs at the Joy Company, a ministry to High-Schools, run and are fully attended. These young people come faithfully because they want to be leaders in their schools and in their future jobs. We just graduated another twenty-two, and their parents attended the graduation, also, my times to teach at the city schools will resume as well. Of course, my job at CRU continues and is always a blessing and challenge to me.

We had a wonderful graduation ceremony at the Joy Co. at the end of July. Each of the 22 graduates came forward and gave their testimony of what they have learned in their class and what they hope to do with that. It is truly amazing how the Lord is leading them, and they love the Bible studies we give. I have become a mentor for four of our girls at Joy Co and I love being a spiritual influence on them.

Since my own four children have built their families, I can meet with them whenever possible, and they encourage my ministries.

There was a little jealousy at the start because in my concern for my students messed-up lives I talked about them more than was necessary. However soon my children realized how needed my help is and they calmed down and enjoyed it with me.

My husband had just left our four children and I and I did not have the courage to tell my daughters yet why dad had not come home at night. It was not possible for me to approach this God I had heard about, because I was scared of Him, being sure that He was punishing me for never acknowledging Him. My daughters had run away from home, and I felt useless and unworthy of even raising my two little sons.

My emotions were out of control, and I switched from being angry to feeling depressed. After feeding my two little boys in the morning, I just went back to bed dwelling on my rejection. There was real insecurity in dealing with everyday life and knowing how to raise my children alone, so I just wanted to shut it all out of my mind rather than dealing with it. Having made a suicide plan, I was not able to carry it out and continued with my depressions.

CALLING OUT FOR HELP

One weekend, my mother in-law picked up my boys to buy them some shoes. I was alone and overwhelmed from the pain, I dropped to the floor crying for a long time. Finally, I yelled out to a God I was not sure existed, to prove Himself and help us. Suddenly, there was an unusual peace in me, and it was on the following day that this God of mercy and love brought about my Salvation. Having lost my car and therefore my job, I took my makeup kit and on a very hot July day and walked to my assigned territory. A young lady answered the first door I knocked on and offered me a cold glass of water.

Giving her my name, she said that she just moved into town and was on staff with Campus Crusade for Christ. Telling her why I was on foot, she asked if I would like to give this trouble into the hands of a God who loves me. Admitting not knowing what she was talking about, she reached for a little yellow booklet called "Do you know the Four Spiritual Laws?" Asking if she could share it with me, I agreed because she had been so kind.vv

This began an unbelievable time of getting to know a God full of mercy, love and compassion, that kept drawing my children and I closer to Himself. Even in trials and sorrows His presence taught us to trust Him because He would see us through. No one could have told us about the deep love this Savior has for those who believe in Him and trust that He gave His life for payment of their sins. However, we learned that soon when we joined the Bible teachings at our church.

Wanting my sons to learn to more about this God we had just come to know, I enrolled them in AWANA, a church youth program for students of all ages. Not wanting to be home alone, I signed up as teachers for the Jr High girls and truly enjoyed it. The job was to listen to their Scripture verses and record their earned points, for which they would receive an award pin for their uniform. To encourage my girls team, I also did the memory craft which became a real joy. I was able to hear my two sons verses and they tested mine, which we liked doing without being competitive.

Attending Community Church became such a blessing and place of growing spiritually till five years later the boys and I moved up to the mountains. Once again, our Lord was so faithful and we fellowshipped in a good Bible teaching church which had a similar Youth Club where the three of us could be active. We only went down to the valley to visit with our family every other weekend, the opposite one they came up to see us, which they loved. Well, seven years later, first Steve and a year after that Bill went into the Service and it was too hard for me to live up there alone. So, with a sad heart because of the empty nest and leaving my mountains, I came back down to the valley.

A NEW MINISTRY BEGAN

Four years have passed now, only the memories without the pain are left, and God, as usual, has brought something beautiful out of all that hurt and loneliness. A neighbor got me involved in a ministry at the Juvenile Detention Center called Juvenile Hall and I received some powerful training. When one of the Bible teachers moved away, he challenged me to take on his Unit. Sensing my Savior's approval, I agreed and two weeks later got started at the city's Youth Prison.

It was an unbelievable time of getting to know my God and learning to believe in His deep love for me by letting me teach these troubled youths. Having shared all my beloved God brought about in five books so far, is a true miracle to me. I had always been an introvert since my husband left our children and me, so now I had fun being able to share what my Savior had done by using me. No longer being afraid of the future gave me the desire to lead others to this wondrous Creator.

At the time my children's father died, I desperately needed a job, and the Lord provided me one at Campus Crusade for Christ in June of 1977. This became a real satisfaction and joy in my life.

I never knew who told them about me but knew Who arranged it for me and was so grateful. I worked at the beautiful Arrowhead Springs Hotel located on the foot of the San Bernardino mountains and I loved my daily rides to work and home.

My beloved Creator had planned in advance for my upcoming pain of the empty nest by giving me 90 children a week at Juvenile Hall and then 10 more on visiting day on the weekend. The sadness gave way to new knowledge and a deeper love and commitment to this awesome God through an additional Bible time at my church. In the meantime, I had received two more grandchildren which used up some of my time and brought more joy into my life through their wonderful presence.

A SINNER, BUT FORGIVEN

Lying was something that came very easy to me, I would be in a conversation and before being aware of it, a lie had once again come out of my mouth. Not being a Christian, it did not bother me much, it was common. However, once I belonged to God, there was a new awareness of it and my enemy used it every way possible.

So, when I read in Isaiah 59:2, "But your iniquities have separated you from your God, and your sins have hidden His face from you so that He will not hear" I was heartbroken. After reading this, being surely convicted, my Creator showed me the seven things that are an abomination to Him in Proverbs, I was shocked. Trying hard to repent and seeking a new way to follow my God, I realized how much additional time in my Saviors word benefited my walk with Him.

He says in Proverbs 6:17 that one of those hateful things, is a lying tongue, and I cried. Pleading seriously that He would help me not to do this lying again, I checked what abomination means and it says detestable. It would take everything in me to fight this, but with His intervention, I was sure it would be possible.

Of course, when my Savior showed me 2 Corinthians 5:17, my guilt and sorrow were eased. In love He tells me "Therefore, if anyone is in Christ, he is a new creation, old things have passed away, behold, all things have become new." Wow, I was rejoicing for this news, not only did I take not lying seriously now, but my love for Him truly deepened.

I realized that my habit of defending myself, when criticized, had not happened in a while. Another beautiful and helpful teaching came in 2 Corinthians 2:10 which says that when I forgive, He forgives me also, and continues in verse:11, lest Satan should take advantage of us. Wow, this big powerful God has it all covered, and I can live in that wonderful peace Jesus has promised. If the Holy Spirit is my comforter, then I must allow Him to do this and not insult Him by worrying about every problem. That forgiving gave me freedom and my enemy had less chance of putting guilt on me.

MY LIFE HAD BEEN GIVEN MORE PURPOSE.

When my Creator said in Romans 8:28 that "all things work together for good to those who love God, to those who are the called according to His purpose," I had to stop and consider this promise. Since I truly love my God, this meant that all He has done in my life turned out for good, no matter how it seemed at the time. This says that even my painful experiences were allowed for His purpose in me.

Well, then I must admit, that it was all worth it, and none of that time was waisted, because I got to know this awesome God. Now I can think of His past instructions in a new way, and continue in confidence, because He promises that He will never change. Jesus prayed to the Father for us, saying in John 17 : !7, " Sanctify them by Your truth, Your word is truth. As You sent Me into the world, I also sent them into the world."

My God sending me into the world was a surprise and a never to be forgotten adventure. There are many pictures and videos to remember them by. As you know, my first mission trip was to

Russia, and I recall standing on a famous hill, overlooking the city of Moscow. Tears came to my eyes, remembering all the bad news reports being told that this is enemy territory. Yet my experiences here were totally different.

Our team got to know the people as kind and very hospitable. The teachers we worked with could not believe that they were told we were their enemies. Each one in our team had ten to twelve teachers in their group. At the end of our weekly training sessions, we hugged and cried, them thanking us wholeheartedly for bringing God back to them. This was very meaningful to us, and we thanked God with all our heart for that blessed opportunity.

I shared in my first book how one of my teacher groups in the Ukraine wrote a song for me to share with the rest of our US trainers. It said how grateful they were to us for sharing the good news with them after seventy years of not being allowed to even mention Him. In short it said that they were lonely and afraid of life without God, but then we came across the Ocean to share the knowledge of God, and now they believe. .

THE SAVIOR REJOICES WITH EVERY NEW CONVERT.

One of my teachers was turning fifty, she and her husband were raising thirty orphans plus their own five children. My interpreter and I were invited to her birthday party, together with about twenty of her friends. We just loved how they sang in their Russian dialect and danced for my co-worker and me.

Their entertainment came after they enjoyed some glasses of Vodka, and their offered friendships seemed real and we responded back. It was something we will never forget. Thousands of these precious teachers prayed to receive Jesus Christ as their Lord and Savior and accepted and used the Bibles we gave them.

Having done this training and Jesus Film showings in several cities in Russia, left us with some great memories and new emotions. With that deep impression left in my mind and heart, I was not able to stop praying for them. Wherever my Lord sent me, I volunteered when some missionaries were needed in one of the Jesus Film Project.

Knowing that my beloved Savior rejoiced as these precious new ones, or sometimes returning children, were saved from the enemy. My friends had warned my director about letting me go on this first mission trip, telling him that I would not stop, and they were proven right. Being half German and half Polish, my adventurous spirit had been many times to Austria and one year to Switzerland.

However, these mission travels awakened a different spirit. Having the blessed purpose of taking the Word of God, left such meaningful impressions and memories. The desire to see more countries did not come until I had been to Russia. This experience of introducing that many people to the God I had come to love, left the desire to continue.

THE BLESSED ADVENTURES CONTINUE.

S ince my children had started families of their own, and I knew that the Lord was in control, my enjoyment of these ministries was unhindered. This first trip was such an unusual and adventurous experience it brought about a longing for more. So, since the Jesus Film's popularity increased so fast, more staff were being needed for the showing of it, so here were my chances.

I loved volunteering and the next opportunity was in the Ukraine, which is next to Poland, the country with the other half of my DNA. My father and his family were Polish, so I got to experience some customs and dishes from his mom, my grandma. I truly enjoyed that country, it reminded me much of my youth in Germany, and the kind and laid-back people before the war.

Many of the teachers and us felt like we had known each other before and admitted the same concerns about home and children and jobs. They had the same love for their country as we did for ours, and I loved those forests of Birch trees like I had grown up nearby. Bringing the life changing knowledge of this awesome, loving and powerful God to them was such a privilege, especially since they were so thankful.

These training sessions were put together so wise, asking them to commit their lives to a God who would not only forgive the past but guide and reward the future. Nothing was ever forced but only offered. The Jesus Film was shown at the beginning of each training session, it always loosened the tight atmosphere and so many gave their lives to the Savior. There is no way I could ever explain thankfulness for wonderful communications with people we had never met before.

These precious teachers blessed us as much as we blessed them and so many agreed that we would look for each other when we were finally in heaven. The only hard thing when we came back home was realizing how grateful they were for things that we took for granted and were so common to us here. We promised to try thanking our God more often and even for the smaller things He so faithfully gave us. It makes us feel a little more at ease in receiving His gifts and enjoying them.

GETTING THE COURAGE AND BOLDNESS TO FOLLOW MY GOD

Falling in love with and teaching on Isaiah 52 made me more courageous and caring less about other people's negative opinions. It says so boldly in Isaiah 43:2 "When you pass through the waters, I will be with you, and through the rivers, they shall not overflow you. When you walk through the fire, you shall not be burned, nor shall the flame scorch you. For I am the Lord your God, the Holy One of Israel, your Savior."

Oh, I loved teaching on that awesome message from this God of love, Who saved me from eternal death. You see my brothers and sisters, I believe very strongly that when I entered the family of God through Salvation, I was grafted into the true olive tree,(being Jesus). Now I can take from that healing sap and get strength to follow His lead.

So, to continue with Isaiah :43, I realize that this is speaking about the old and the new Israel, I felt part of all this when My Father says in verse 7, "Everyone who is called by My name, whom I have created for My glory, I have formed him, yes, I have made him."

This made me sure that the Gentiles were part of those beautiful promises, and I became bolder in my faith and my testimony. There was no more fear because I am totally convinced that I am called by His name, and He even now still forms me by a greater knowledge of Him.

Therefore, I began to use just what my Creator has given me and stop trying to copy and imitate other people I admired. Whatever this beloved Savior has told me to do, He has always provided for, and I never had to walk in shame. Being authentic means being the same whether no one sees me, or I am out in public.

This way I can live in the peace my Savior promises in John 14:26-27, "peace I leave with you, My peace I give to you, not as the world gives, give I unto you." In His loving way this Savior continues "let not your heart be troubled, neither let it be afraid."

IS IT TIME TO COME HOME SOON?

T his way and with other promises like these, my beloved God encouraged me, and I did not give up. Having lived with this Creator God all these years, has kept my enemy at a safe distance, unless my old self gave him an opportunity. However, spending time in God's precious Word greatly limited the evil influence. This is one of the many blessings from being in the Word.

Almost from the beginning, as soon as I was convinced that I was truly saved, my longing was to be with my beloved God. Having had some real heartbreaking situations in my live, surrendering to this God of love changed the lives of my four children and me forever. Having this Savior bring my entire family into the kingdom greatly relieved my concern about them not being left behind.

I needed to be sure they would go up to Him when He comes for His own. This merciful God I have come to know and love back, has shared with us some of His awesome work as examples.

One of the reports I use in my teachings is the story of Ruth. Having lost her husband, she decided not to go back to her family but stay with her mother-in-law. Through her faithfulness and hard work God rewarded her with a new husband and baby boy named Obed. Even her mother-in-law, who had lost her husband and two sons, found a new reason for living.

One of my other favorites is the story of Joshua and the way the Lord told him, as He did me, do not fear. This comes up in the Bible 365 times, once for every day, wow. Joshua, as I did, learned soon how very trustworthy this God is and began to be obedient to His advice and instructions. Finding out that blessings come with obedience made it easier to follow His commands and discover that they were for the believer's benefit.

MORE GREAT EXAMPLES

Another lady, her name was Rahab, took in and hid the spies Joshua sent to check out Jericho. Because of this, she and her family were saved when the walls came down. Here is another Gentile that entered the blood line of Jesus because of His great mercy. It gave the Gentiles hope for Salvation, then, as it does now.

This awesome God has so many stories and examples in His precious book to give His children hope. The reason these wonderful stories were given to us, was to show us the great mercy and love our heavenly Father has for those who are His. There is no partiality with Him, His love is the same for all the believers.

The Bible tells us the Devil roams around like a roaring lion in 1 Peter 5:8, to seek whom he may devour. I thank my Savior with all my heart that this is no longer a fear because Jesus defeated Satan forever by His death. Now, I am careful not to give this enemy an opportunity to trip me up, or to fall for his deceptive temptations. I give thanks and praises for all He suffered to save me.

Wanting to be authentic and not knowing what the word really means, "Googling" was my best solution. It told me: it means genuine, undisputed, real. This is what God's word, the Bible is to me, the only two words I would add is absolute truth. This is what I desire to have described to me, to be genuine, real, truthful, and this is what I ask my beloved Creator for.

When problems come, I must not pretend they do not exist, just be at peace, knowing Who will take care of it all . Being authentic and trusting in this world is what my Savior desires, and that is what will be my goal. Having asked my Lord to give me the things He wants me to share, He truly answered. Being amazed, I just do what He brings to my consciousness. It seems I cannot stop, so with great joy I continue.

ALWAYS HOLD FAST THIS PRECIOUS WORD

Sometimes, while reading this love letter God has written to His children, my thoughts are suddenly somewhere else. Saying I am sorry, brings me back for a while, however it will happen again, and I hate it. Laying my Bible aside for a little and just being still and listening, the Holy Spirit will clear my mind of unimportant clutter.

Now that I am mature (that sounds better than being old), I hope my children will remember the times that I did not take away their privileges or did not punish them. Wanting them to recall our church times, Saturday evening movies and dinners at church, and youths' conferences, so they will always walk with this faithful, loving God.

Claiming, Proverbs 22:6 "Train up a child in the way he should go and when he is old, he will not depart from it" every day and having posted it in a frame on the wall, should still be on their mind now . Also, where it says in Proverbs 13:24 "he who spares his rod, hates his son, but he who loves him is diligent to discipline him."

This is one of the reasons, I love my God with all my heart, because of the way He gave me what was needed to finish raising my four children. He also impressed me to hold fast to the faithful Word, studying it seriously, obeying it as possible and to share it with others in confidence.

I can apply this Word at any time by letting it influence me, and using it to win, while seeking my Savior's will for my life. I thank my precious supporters often for sending me to teach God's word to those who don't know Him. Ever since my Savior redeemed me and made me His, I longed to be with Him.

A HARD CHOICE TO MAKE

Agreeing with Paul in one thing however, how He put it so well in Philippians 1:21 For to me, to live is Christ, and to die is gain. However, he continues in verse :23 for I am hard-pressed between the two, having a desire to depart and be with Christ, which is far better. And then he says in verse :24 nevertheless to remain in the flesh is more needful for you.

So, I agreed with Paul, and even though my own four children were saved, there were still a few of my family not His yet. Getting to work on it by bringing them before my loving God daily, asking Him to show them their need of Him. Sad to say, the rest did not let me talk about my God until eight years later, but then they came into the kingdom one after the other.

When my stubborn little mom, being the last, got baptized, I thanked my God in tears. Satan will do whatever he can to take praise and glory away from God. That is why I try hard, making sure that I do not take credit for what my God does through me. I must give thanks and honor to my beloved Savior.

He has always supplied all the needs for my children and me and has taken care of my grandchildren and great grandchildren, as well as all those in-laws as they have joined us. Being greatly encouraged by my Creator's wonderful promises, and the stories of Him caring for all these people, I knew He would take care of them.

In Philippians 4:19 it says so beautifully, "And my God shall supply all my needs according to His riches in glory by Christ Jesus." It would have been an insult to Him if I would have been worried about their situations, except to help in a true emergency. Even then only with the Lord's approval and He always came through.

WHOSE FAULT IS IT ANYWAY

When I went through a storm, before complaining, I tried to make sure the one that got me into it was not me. I am hoping to say in those days, as Paul said, "I have fought the good fight, I have finished the race, I have kept the faith." It really seemed that the storms got shorter that way.

When I go to the beach or park, I like to pass out those precious booklets like the one I was saved by. Yesterday, there were nine people taking the booklets, I was content and went back to my friend's house to spend a peaceful evening. So many of these promises have given me courage and sometimes also guilt.

It says in Romans 5:5 with truth, "Now hope does not disappoint, because the love of God has been (past) poured out in our hearts, by the Holy Spirit, who has been (past) given to us." This tells me that this special love of God is already in me, it means, that it is up to me to use it when needed.

It also says to me, that I do not need to plead with my Savior to give me love for anyone, He tells me that the love is already in me, it is therefore my choice to use it. This means, when someone just said something mean or unkind to me, I can surprise them with a kind answer and maybe share God's love with them.

Perhaps I can even lead them to this awesome Creator to be saved and brought into the kingdom. Not knowing when He has planned this, makes me responsible to be aware of who comes into my life each day instead of just paying attention to what my own desires are.

IT IS THE SPIRIT WHO GIVES LIFE

Being thankful for this new life given to me means I need to know what my Savior gave it to me for. He says to me in John 6:63, " It is the Spirit who gives life, the flesh profits nothing. The words that I speak to you are spirit, and they are life." This should make me be more aware of His warnings, not only His promises.

The Bible is a mirror that shows me what my life should be like after walking with this gracious, patient God. I should no longer need milk but be ready for some healthy empowering feeding. As I have shared so many times in my previous five books, nothing is **more** valuable than that precious time in my Father's love letter.

This is the only way I can grow, the only way I can learn to hear the wonderful voice of my God. Having always heard that the fruits of the Spirit are, love, joy, peace, longsuffering, kindness, goodness, faithfulness, gentleness, self-control, I did not like to hear it too much because I did not possess any of them fully, only each of them partial.

This means also my perfection is far off and much work is still needed. However, when I get discouraged, my beloved Savior reminds me how far I have come and that He is not with me any less than before. This Creator-Savior reminds me that I am a new creation now, and declares in 1 Corinthians 6:17, that he who is joined to the Lord is one spirit with Him.

But an even more powerful and blessing word is the one in 1 John 4:17, "Love has been perfected among us in this, that we may have boldness in the day of judgement, because as He is, so are we in this world." There is unbelievable comfort in this promise, because we do not have to be afraid when judgement comes, because, as Our Savior is, so are we in this world. It says clearly, so we are, not so we should <u>be.</u>

HIS FAITHFULNESS NEVER LEAVES US

E ven remembering the time, being in Germany during World War II, and the suffering of my mom with us three girls, my being eight at the end. Someone had to be protecting us, though we did not know yet that it was God. There being much death and hunger, there were also miracles that had to be admitted and could not be denied.

There were three very specific times where we escaped certain death and we thanked a God we were told existed but had not revealed Himself to us yet. Not until we had been in America through my marriage to an American soldier, and some unbelievable pain, that this awesome God became reality.

It says so clear and comforting in Philippians 4:6 and :7 "Be anxious for nothing but in everything by prayer and supplication, with thanksgiving, let your request be made known to God, and the peace of God which surpasses all understanding, will guard your hearts and minds through Christ Jesus."

I am so grateful that my Lord's commands and promises are clear and understandable, and they guard my heart and mind so I can know that they are from Him. In my blessed work with

Campus Crusade for Christ, for all these 45 years and all my trips and ministries, I have never lacked anything in comparison to the "before Christ" days.

Having always trusted in the Matthew 6:33 promise, by seeking my Father's kingdom first, everything I needed was always provided for me and my children. Sometimes in food and closing and sometimes in a car or refrigerator, sometimes in school supplies or mountain bicycles for my boys. Do you remember my sharing all these stories?

Having always prayed for my kids *having* Christian friends who will turn them back if they go the wrong way, He answered. My son Steve had a Christian roommate who got him out of trouble when left without a ride to the Army base, and my son Bill found a relative he had never met before when needing a place to live and to worship.

HIS FAITHFULNESS NEVER ENDS

It was the same with these many overseas trips, I had to raise my own funds, the money always came in, mostly more than needed, my Lord always supplied. The ministry and trips were truly a success and blessing, which made me look forward to the next one. Learning to trust my Creator was a never to be forgotten experience and will stay with me always.

Enjoying Romans 6:17 and :18, which tells me "God be thanked, that though you were slaves of sin, yet you obeyed from the heart that form of doctrine to which you are delivered. So, having been set free from sin, you became slaves of righteousness." He has never once let me down but was faithful to His word.

There is no way I could possibly recall all the times, especially since most of the time I was not even aware of His gifts or helps. I was usually so busy enjoying live with my Savior, which made me ignorant to dangers or unaware of bad attitudes toward me. Mainly because I took His promises of protection seriously.

Wow, that is a beautiful promise, in verse :22, "having been set free from sin, and having become slaves of God, you have your fruit to holiness, and the end, everlasting life." This is so awesome,

I do not have to live in constant fear of this enemy persuading me to follow his deceitfulness but my assurance is the faithfulness of my God.

The troubles of the past were needed to bring me to my turning point and my acceptance of a Savior. Whenever I am in a storm, rather than complaining or accusing, I learned to find out who got me into it. If it turns out it was me, a quiet retreat is the humblest move. I pray at that time "Lord, lift me higher, closer to You, make me more useable."

That prayer usually got answered and all was at peace again. There is no use trying to shift the guilt to someone else, the truth will always come out. Knowing that I am loved and have my future secured overcomes everything. There were more times I had to practice patience than comes to remembrance, but what I can recall, it always brought rewards.

ONE OF THE GREATEST ANSWERS

The longest answer to prayer came after 51 years, but when it came was worth the wait. What it says in Philippians 4:13 "I can do all things in Christ who strengthens me" is true. However, this one involved a close family relationship, so I just had to wait and trust. But the making up was so sweet I would wait for it again.

This answer had to do with my daughter Christina, who allowed the enemy to persuade her that it was my fault that her dad left us, even though she knew the truth. There was no one else available to be blamed and my girl was hurting. God was not in our lives yet, but it would not be long before that miracle occurred.

That new Helper, which Jesus said the Father would send, is truly an unbelievable gift and He helps me do what I could never accomplish alone. Therefore, that beautiful day came when Christina said that she loves me, and a new friendship began for her and me. This way of life will remain until our beloved God takes us home.

Truth is also a precious gift because it is my Savior Jesus Christ, that claims in John 14:6 saying, "I am the way, the truth and the life, no one comes to the Father but by Me." Only through Him can I come to the Father which happened, which means soon we will be face to face. It looks like this is the time of the harvest, because it feels strongly like the time for His return.

There is a precious parable Jesus told where a man sowed good seed in Matthew 13:24, but while he slept his enemy sowed tares. So, when the wheat sprouted, the tares also grew. But when his servants asked to gather up the tares, the owner said no, verse :29 "lest while you gather the tares you also uproot the wheat with them."

I WILL COME AGAIN

This is so important at harvest time, when I was young, I got to live among acers of vegetables, and we were careful not to pull too many weeds. It seemed just like Jesus said, we did not want to harm the good ones so, sometimes, we had to leave the bad ones until the harvest.

The Lord was saying, live amongst the unbelievers until He comes and gathers His children to their home, as He promised in John 14:3 that we will be where He is. There is another story in Revelation 14:14 were John said he saw a cloud and there sat One like the Son of man having on His head a golden crown, and in His hand a sharp sickle.

And another angel came out and cried with a loud voice "Trust in Your sickle and reap for the time has come for You to reap, for the harvest of the earth is ripe. Verse :16 continues "So He who sat on the cloud thrust in His sickle on the earth and the earth was reaped."

As a believer I have always known that there is a time of judgement and I wanted to be ready for it. I made sure the rest of my family was made aware of it, both by me and our churches.

It was too hard to think of any of them left behind, even though most my teachings were about this God of love who wanted us with Him forever.

Yet I always snug in the warnings now and then, so they kept coming to the Bible studies and were made aware of a judgement day and be ready for it. In our study times I saw who was not paying close attention and made sure we had some extra time together. I wanted them to be aware there would be a time of love and rewards but also a judgement.

WHEN A SCRIPTURE JUMPS OUT, CHECK IT

Whenever I read my God's word and a certain verse lights up, I stop and read it a few times and find out if the Spirit is telling me something. This is another way my beloved Father speaks and if I ask, He will confirm it. There is a wonderful encouraging word in Isaiah 30:21 which says, "Your ears shall hear a word behind you, saying 'This is the way, walk in it." This happened whenever I bothered to ask my Savior, if I did not, I was on my own.

My beloved heavenly Father has always shown me one step at a time so I would not get scared of give up before it was done. Isaiah said in chapter 42:16 so powerfully, "I will bring the blind by a way they did not know; I will lead them in paths they have not known. I will make darkness light before them, and crooked places straight. These things I will do for them, and not forsake them." This felt like it was written for me because I was blind and in darkness when Jesus called me.

God will open my eyes at the right time for something He

wants me to do and He will have given me the needed knowledge and equipment already. There will be no confusion about the where or when or how, He will make it clear, He is faithful in that. It was hidden from me, even if I read it before, but at the right time it will make sense. If it is my idea, He will make it known in His right timing.

Both my sons and I experienced this when I put our house up for sale because we wanted to move to the Colorado mountains. I had sent out job resumes to Christian Ministries in Colorado Springs. This generous Lord gave us a motorhome and on Easter Sunday in 1984 we headed out to live in the Colorado mountains. We had asked our God to give us that mountainous state. We found a place to live, and I interviewed for a job with a Christian Ministry.

Well, when we got there, we liked it, but it was not what we wanted. Our desire was to live in the mountains, however there was only one city in the mountains, it was Estes Park. It would have been a two-and-a-half-hour drive down to my job and after work the same back home. The drive would be all up hill and, in the winter, usually snowed in.

This ministry was going to wait for me two months, but my home would not sell. So, they had to hire someone else, and we found out that our Lord wanted us in the San Bernardino mountains. I stayed with Campus Crusade for Christ and as soon as we agreed to this, our house sold. We found a perfect place and two weeks later we were moving into our California mountain home.

THIS JESUS WILL COME BACK AS HE LEFT

When Jesus left the earth, He said that He is going to prepare a place for us in John 14:3, "and if I go and prepare a place for you, I will come again and receive you to Myself, that where I am, there you may be also." This I truly look forward to and can hardly wait for it, but while He has me here, I will be obedient to His plan for me.

Sharing His amazing plan and deep love for His believers is always my joy. It is amazing that the two angels said that He will come back exactly the way He left. Our Savior made it all clear to us, so we can tell others about this awesome plan He and the Father had set up for His children. This is why it is written in Romans 13:11, "And do this, knowing the time, that now it is high time to awake out of sleep, for now our Salvation is nearer than when we first believed."

Paul suggested that we put on the armor of light, and this applies much more to us than it did to them. So, I stop complaining and focus on saving others, rather than what condition the world is in. I can do something about the first but can do nothing about the world, however I will pray and vote. Knowing God's plans and what He wants me to do, and my part in it, is easier to find out than what the world is going to do next.

In the meantime, I will continue to live by what my Lord told me in Isaiah 54:4 to :6, "For your Maker is your husband, the Lord of hosts is His name, and your Redeemer is the Holy One of Israel, He is called the God of the whole earth. For the Lord has called you like a woman forsaken and grieved in spirit, like a youthful wife when you were refused, says your God."

This Maker and Redeemer, continues in verse :13 " All your children shall be taught by the Lord, and great shall be the peace of your children." His promise continues so powerfully in verse :17 "No weapon formed against you shall prosper and every tongue which rises against you in judgement you shall condemn. This is the heritage of the servants of the Lord, and their righteousness is from Me," says the Lord.

FALLING FOR THIS SAVIOR WAS SO EASY AND LASTING

I could not possibly share with you what a blessing and comfort this Scripture was to this forsaken, lost and lonely single mom. When I read this the first time my tears just flowed as my heart fell hook, line and sinker for this God who loves me like this. My heart has never left Him for a moment since then, but it grew closer with every one of those thousands of promises He wrote to His children in His love letter.

Whenever I ministered to someone depressed or afraid, the most encouraging and promising Scriptures I used are in Isaiah 43: 2 "When you pass through the waters, I will be with you, and through the rivers, they shall not overflow you. When you walk through the fire, you shall not be burned, nor shall the flame scorch you."

Once again, I thought this was only for Israel in the beginning, until I read in verse :7 "Everyone who is called by My name, whom I have created for My glory, I have formed him, yes, I have made him." These words have always been so uplifting and encouraging to me and they let me press forward to find out my Saviors next plans.

All these years I had the Holy Spirit to teach me and guide me in the things I was told to do, and I could use what I had been given. Since He knows my future, He has always let me know what is next, mostly at the last moment so I cannot interfere. Only I can stop His precious work in me, so I am very careful to pay attention to His word and His voice.

THIS TIME THE LORD WAS MOST REAL

One of the times His presence was very clear and visible was at my car-accident in Kentucky. Even though I shared the details in my third book, I want to make the unbelievable planning of it aware. A family member and I had just come back to my son's house and had pulled into his driveway.

Suddenly there was a tremendous impact and pain in my body as a car hit the passenger side I was seated in. This car had come off the road, across the yard in order to hit us. I will never know how my son's fire department arrived this fast. Finding myself squeezed tightly in my seat and covered with hundreds of pieces of glass,I had trouble breathing.

The fireman on my left informed me that the only way to get all that glass of me was to cut open the left side of my dress to roll the glass off. They covered me quickly and started to slide me down out of the seat. My son Bill was a member of this fire department, and I knew he was praying. The next thing I was aware of was being in an ambulance with an IV in each of my arms and hearing the sirens.

The transfer to the hospital in Lexington should have been

1 ½ hours but was only 45 minutes because of the sirens and lights. I had always wondered if I would be angry with my God if something really bad would happen to me. Gratefully I realized, that I was praising my Creator the entire long ride to the hospital, thanking Him for His strong presence with me.

After one initial surgery to fix my cracked pelvis in three places, there were no additional ones. The two months in the hospital, were spent waiting for all my cracked ribs to heal, so physical therapy was hard but walking again was said to be impossible.

MY GOD'S AWESOME PLANNING

The fireman team my son belongs to that if she had hit our car one foot more to the front I would not have survived. They said that my whole pelvis would have been crushed. The other problem was that a part of the doorframe had broken off over my head would have entered my skull. This was an unusual happening and the police said that her brakes were never touched. So, my enemy wanted me out of his way, but my father said NO!

My beloved daughter in law had turned my case over to a lawyer in her church and requested a settlement. Not having known you can do anything like that, I thanked her and waited to see the outcome. I had been asking my Lord to let my home and car be paid off, but could not imagine how this could be done. The settlement I received was enough to pay off my home and car and I truly praised my God.

When I dwell on the way my Lord had planned my life, despite my wrong choices, my amazement never ends. By saving my life in the WWII war in Germany many times, to stopping my suicide, I am so grateful. There is no way to count all the other times of His intersession, because He knew someday, I would say "yes" to Him.

It says in Ephesians 1:4 and :5, "just as He chose us in Him (Jesus) before the foundation of the world, that we should be holy and without blame before Him in love, having predestined us to adoption as sons by Jesus Christ to Himself, according to the good pleasure of His will." What an awesome promise!

Even after my birth, He had to wait another 37 years before I gave my life to this very patient God of love. Judging by the past I can totally trust Him with my future and will continue reading His life-giving word and wait for His voice. My Savior says so kindly in John 15:3, "you are already clean because of the word which I have spoken to you."

So, cleaning is another precious thing His word does for us. This wonderful God tells us in Romans 5:1, "Therefore, having been justified (declared not guilty) by faith, we have peace with God through our Lord Jesus Christ." It continues in verse :2, "through Whom also we have access by faith into this grace in which we stand." This grace is a special gift from our Savior which He earned by His death.

THE MOVE TO FOLLOW MY BELOVED JESUS FILM

The ten years I lived in San Clemente, was a very special time and the knowledge of my beloved Lord was greatly increased. My God had me continue giving Bible studies in the Juvenile Detention Center in the city of Orange and give Sunday School classes to the high school age youth at my church. other

Missing my families so much I drove 1 ½ hours one way to be with them every weekend. The church I attended while being home, was the one my youngest son and his family belonged to. They were planning to start a high school youth group and I was asked to help the youth-pastor teach this group when I was there every other weekend.

When one of my grandsons joined the Marines at Camp Pendleton Base, I went to visit him there. We would have a light snack and study the Bible in my van. Soon, one and then three of his friends joined us in this which I loved. I asked My Savior to work it out to where I could give Bible studies to many more of the young Marines.

The ones who staffed the Bases in California were the Navigators and meeting with them, I got permission to give Bible studies there. Now I had to find somewhere on the Base to give these studies in. Remembering seeing a big YMCA building on the Base, I met with the director.

The Lord worked it out where I could give my studies in that huge hall which had lots of chairs and an enormous TV. Only two young soldiers came the first night, 14 the second and 32 the third night. Depending on which companies had come back to the Base, showed how many young soldiers would attend the Bible study that week.

Soon my young men asked if I could give study a second night and I received the permission. My Guys asked for a third night, and it was allowed also. However, when they wanted a fourth night, the YMCA said no because the rest of the nights they had their own programs.

Those Bible studies were awesome and lasted three nights a week, three hours each night and my young soldiers were serious about them, no playing around. These Bible times continued on the weekends when seven of my students got to be at my home. This was all I could fit in my van. They were so grateful not having to go with the rest of their buddies to the city were the temptations were free and easy.

SO ALL CAN HEAR HIS MESSAGE OF LOVE

Loving the teaching of my Fathers word, He trusted me with more and soon came another chance I would never have imagined. One of the scriptures much on my mind was Romans 10:13-15, where it says, "For whoever calls on the name of the Lord shall be saved. How then shall they call on Him in whom they have not believed?

And how shall they believe in Him of whom they have not heard? And how shall they hear without a preacher? And how shall they preach unless they are sent?" As it is written: "How beautiful are the feet of those who preach the Gospel of peace, who bring glad tidings of good things!"

This is one of the scriptures I send my precious supporters the start of every year to tell them of my gratefulness for sending me. Having been always ashamed of my big feet, my mom always told me that at being 6 ½ feet tall, I would not be able to keep my balance if I had small feet.

However, when I was finally a Christian and read Romans 10:15, I was glad that my feet were big and were beautiful to God. There was so much that changed when my beloved Savior entered my life, and I have tried and prayed that I would never go back to the old ways.

Having been attached to the true vine for 48 years now, has been real peace and joy, and I will do anything to show someone that beautiful way to this God of love. Not being able to remember my life without my Savior except when I am writing, is a gift from Him, because now I can dwell on my future instead.

ALWAYS PROTECTED, NEVER ALONE

B eing in touch with this gracious God every day is so beneficial because it helps me truly to be aware when the enemy tries his lies and tricks. It is so assuring to know how my Savior feels about certain actions and attitudes I had developed in the past. They did not show His uplifting way of life and now the Holy Spirit helps me to, little by little, change them.

My greatest desire in this life is to take my family and **all** I pray for daily, up with me to heaven and have none of them left behind. Only the classes I teach the Bible to I will pray for as a group, and I think of them much. Asking my heavenly Father to give them His wisdom and keep them from the evil one brings me peace.

All those years the Lord used me in the Juvenile Detention Center I came to love many of my young student and longed to stay in touch with a few especially needful ones. The only way I was allowed to do this was by being ordained. So, after 1 1/2 years of training, Campus Crusade for Christ had me ordained.

Now I could see them on the outside but only if the youths were given the ok by the Probation Department. These young people were taught from Luke 10:19, that Jesus gave us authority over all the power of the enemy, and nothing would in any way hurt us. This meant they needed to be in close contact with their Lord and Savior.

Since their Lord had saved them, they had to be sure of their position in Christ to use this authority He would give to them. I love that Scripture and remind Satan of it many times. The Bible also tells us in Luke 10:21, "In that hour Jesus rejoiced in the Spirit and said, "I thank you Father, Lord of heaven and earth, that you have hidden these things from the wise and prudent and revealed them to babes."

NO MORE DARK DAYS, THE TEARS ARE GONE

The beloved Father has shown these things to us so we can walk in strong faith, giving our enemy very rare opportunities to deceive us. The Savior said in John 14:19, "A little while longer and the world will see Me no more, but you will see Me. Because I live you will live also." Wow, with this assurance we can surely know and depend on our beloved Creator's future and plans for us.

"At that day you will know that I am in My Father and you in Me, and I in you." Jesus could not have made it any clearer what our position is in Him and in the Father. One of the things He assured us of is that He is in us and that we will live. These beautiful promises continue because He knows that His children need to be assured of His constant presence.

Being convinced that He has forgiven and forgotten my sins, as He promised, I can now focus on Him guiding me to reach those who need Him. He says so comfortably in Matthew 11:28, "Come to Me, all you who labor and are heavy laden, and I will give you rest." I keep hoping and waiting for that rest He promises.

He continues in verse :29, "take My yoke upon you and learn from Me, for I am gentle and lowly in heart, and you will find rest for your souls." I have never found any human being promise anything like that, probably because no one would be able to make, much less keep such a promise.

Having been able to totally trust my God with all these thousands of promises, it has been a joy to live in the knowledge of them by being so often in that blessed Word. It was about a year after falling in the waiting arms of my merciful God that I realized that my crying had stopped and there was this indescribable peace.

There was no more the feeling of getting even or hurting back, only this unusual quiet in me. The only reason I can have it is because of that precious time in my Saviors word, that loving letter He wrote to the believers He loves so much. He means for that to be a steady reality to those He loves.

It kept reminding me of the story of Jacob, now called Israel, and his brother Esau. I would have thought that Esau wanted to still kill his brother, like he had planned to in the beginning. Who changed Esau's mind, could it have been God, the God who hated Esau? We have to be in our new body before we can truly know our beloved Lord.

OUR FATHER ALWAYS HAS THE PERFECT PLAN

I srael was sure that his brother was coming to kill him. That is why he sent ahead some of his wives and children and animals to soothe his brother. God has often used unbelievers to benefit His children before, could that have been the reason for the change of Esau's plan? My Savior says in John 15:2 that every branch that bears fruit He prunes, that it may bear more fruit.

And this awesome God promises in verse :3, "You are already clean because of the word which I have spoken to you." This is another benefit for being in that blessed and encouraging word, I am in its messages daily being refreshed and enlightened. I cannot say that often enough because it has totally changed my life.

This is why the 23 Psalm was such a comfort to me because it promises in verse : 6, that I will live in the house of the Lord forever. This and so many other promises have put me totally at ease about belonging to God forever. Another one is Romans 8:38 and 39 which tells me that nothing and no one can separate me from the love of God. These are only a few of the Scriptures that I repeat and claim for my future.

NOT JUST A NEW BEGINNING BUT A NEW ENDING

I can write a new beginning of my life, and since my Lord saved me, I can now write a new ending of my life. So much has changed for the better and no one and nothing can make me go back to the old. I dwell often on Romans 8:38 and 39 which says that neither death nor life, neither angels nor demons, nor any other created thing shall be able to separate me from the love of God which is in Christ Jesus our Lord.

And since I feel strongly that these are the last days, I like what Ephesians says in chapter 5:4, awake you who sleep, arise from the dead, and Christ will give you light. It goes on in verse :15 do not walk as fools but as wise men, redeeming the time, because the days are evil. This is such good advice and I pray for wisdom for God's people so they will see the tactics of the enemy and stay close to the Father's instructions.

There is just no end to the wisdom given in this precious love letter because the Father did not want His beloved children to fall for the enemies lies and deception. It is why He said in John 14:19,

"A little while longer and the world will see Me no more, but you will see Me. Because I live, you will live also." This is so powerful and comforting but is not all, He continues on with something just as awesome and loving in verse :20, " At that day you will know that I am in My Father, and you in Me and I in you."

WOW, this assured me so totally that I am His and that Satan has no power over me. I will do anything not to give this enemy any opportunity for me to offend my God by being disobedient to His beloved instructions. There is even more assurance in verse :21, "he who has My commandments and keeps them, it is he who loves Me. And he who loves Me will be loved by My Father and I will love him and manifest Myself to him." This is still not the end yet, Jesus wanted us to fully understand where His believers stand.

MY PEACE I GIVE TO YOU

The Savior continues on in verse :23, "If anyone loves Me, he will keep My word, and My Father will love him, and We will come to him and make Our home with him. And in :26, "But the Helper, the Holy Spirit, whom the Father will send in My name, He will teach you all things, and bring to your remembrance all things that I said to you."

Just as beautiful in verse :27, Peace I leave with you, My peace I give to you, not as the world gives to you do I give to you. Let not your heart be troubled, neither let it be afraid. This is all such wonderful conformation which we surely will believe and trust Him with, and yet there is so much more like Romans 6:18, were it says, "and having been set free from sin, you became slaves of righteousness.

With such awesome promises, how could I ever claim not to be able So, this should put away all that guilt the enemy has been trying to lay on me all these years and I can boldly tell him that I have been set free forever. I have been telling him to find another fool who will listen to his lies, my Savior told me that I am no longer under his control, but am a slave of righteousness, Halelujah!

He showed that in order to have that close relationship with Him, I could not have someone or something against me, or me against anyone. The first and most important one was my ex-husband and I had to start there. Matthew 6:15 told me "But if you do not forgive men their trespasses, neither will your Father forgive your trespasses."

There are so many more Scriptures like these, that I got the message. The rest of the people I called said they could not remember anything, and a true feeling of relieve came over me. I cannot remember ever feeling so light and forgiven before and I could not think of anyone else to call that I might have offended.

A BEAUTIFUL FREEDOM

So, I told my Savior that I love Him and went to sleep. The very best advice I could give, is to forgive, even if they say no, your part has been done, you are released, and all is forgiven you. This brings an unbelievable freedom and felt like a heavy weight has come of my shoulders.

There are 50 other verses on forgiveness according to Google, but one I really took seriously was Matthew 5:23 and 24, where it says "Therefore, if you bring your gift to the altar and there remember that your brother has something against you, leave your gift and first be reconciled with your brother and then come and offer your gift."

So, it was obvious how important this is to my Father and I made sure that all was cleared on this subject in my life. Before I share two more Scriptures on forgiveness, I want to give the reason why we should forgive. It says very clearly in 1 John 1:9 "If we confess our sins, He is faithful and just to forgive us our sins and to cleanse us from all unrighteousness."

There is no better reason than this to obey His command, this is not a request, my God is serious about this because He knows what a damage unforgiveness is to my character. Even though there are so many more I would just like to show two more.

One is Ephesians 4:32 which says "And be kind to one another, tenderhearted, forgiving one another, even as God in Christ forgave you." Also, in Luke 6:37 it tells us "judge not and you will not be judged, condemn not and you shall not be condemned, forgive and you will be forgiven."

The last one I want to mention is from the prayer Jesus taught us in Matthew 6:12 "And forgive us our debts **as we** forgive our debtors."

NOTHING HAPPENS WITHOUT HIS PURPOSE

B ecause the absence of meat and milk during the war time, I had very brittle bones. Due to this problem, I had to have both my hips and my left knee replaced. Because this procedure was brand new in the US, I was one of the first people to have these surgeries done.

Sadly, it took nine major surgeries to make it work because my body rejected these large foreign objects, and the pieces would no stay in place but dislocated. The first five operations took place before I had any relationship with the God of heaven. Belonging to Him would have made un unbelievable difference.

The last four surgeries were after my Salvation and were as different as night and day from the ones before Christ. The blessings were all the roommates I got to lead to my beloved Savior. There were such a variety of them and since I had to stay in the hospital three weeks each time, the Lord gave me three roommates for each surgery.

The most unusual one was a lady who had been traveling to

visit a friend. She was in a car accident, was released from the urgent care with pain pills for a headache. They discovered later that day the break in her neck and searched for her everywhere. She was trying to head back home but had to spend another night in a motel because of her bad headache.

She notified her husband who did not get her message until the next day. The medical team was waiting at her home, and immediately put her in a neck brace, called for an ambulance and brought her to the hospital I was located in. When they brought her to my room she was waiting for a larger and more permanent head and neck brace.

I had never seen anything like that nor heard a more unbelievable and sadder story. However, she got to know the Creator of heaven and earth and left a strong believer in Him. There were other stories similar and there were overseas trips with miracles in them, I will tell one of them.

It was in one of the many villages we showed the Jesus Film to in India, it was next to a large Rock Quarry. In most cases both husband and wife worked there while the older children watched the younger ones. There was no school available even though it was sad because these children were bright and noticed everything.

GOD'S HAND IS ON EACH
OF THE SHOWINGS

In these villages, the huts were clean and had circles of rocks for cooking and woven mats for sleeping. Most of the women had gold colored jewelry in their ears and noses and showed off their children. It was so precious to our team that all were really attentive to the Jesus Film and most seemed to say the Salvation prayer at the end of the show.

They always are asked to come the lights afterward and receive a copy of the Gospel of Luke, which the Film was made after. Whenever we asked if they wanted to learn more about this God all the hands went up even though they had the statues of their own gods everywhere.

We did much praying during these showings because these villages have priests who are angry about our visits and often showed it. The members of our team, usually four of us, were aware of the opposition and used extra care and prayers. Almost every showing had a person leave, screaming at the top of their voice. However, we were warned and have seen our God's protection and the power of prayer at these times.

The Jesus Film made by Campus Crusade for Christ has been shown since it's creation in every country of the world. We have the film in over 2,000 languages so far and God had His hand of blessing on it from the very beginning. There have been many oppositions, because Satan hates the film and showed it in many ways.

But as we believers are told in the Bible, greater is He that is in us, than he that is in the world according to 1 John 4:4. We have seen the victories of our Creator so many times and in unbelievable ways, so our fears were very limited. Our entry into one of the countries took so long that it was almost midnight before we were through the check point.

I WILL NEVER LEAVE YOU OR FORSAKE YOU

We had to open each one of our suitcases and the line was unusually long, and we did not know if someone would still be there waiting for us on the other end. So, we began to cross over on a very large, all metal bridge when suddenly it began to shake harder and harder.

There was suddenly a very bright light and we realized that there was a train coming to cross the bridge with us. Moving as far to the edge of the fence as possible, we crossed the bridge very slowly, watching every step since the way was rough and uneven.

By the time we got to the end of our new country, it was after one am and no one was there to pick us up. So, we sat on our suitcases and prayed knowing our God knew all about it. It was one hour later that a van arrived and took us to our quarters. Well, we knew by then that our enemy hated us being there for ten days.

We also experienced our heavenly Father's pleasure for our obedience to His call to this place, and the success in being witnesses for Him was great. One of our staff and I were taken to orphanages every morning to teach English and there were always chances to share about our God, and someone to interpret.

There were no accidents or any kind of mishaps and there could have been, especially automobile ones. The roads were all sand and only the very center of the city was paved. However, the students came faithfully to our English classes, and some received our blessed Savior as their own.

They accepted the Bibles we gave in their language and the parents did not object to it either. It was a never to be forgotten memory and these precious new believers are still in their Saviors arms. All of us, there were seven, were given a rare chance to buy some memorable items to bring home.

However only one letter arrived to me, and it was a thank you for bringing God to them. Telling by our little response cards at least six billion have seen this awesome Film and so many gave their life to this loving Savior. Of course, this is not the end of it yet and we are hoping and praying for so many more.

There is a wonderful verse in 2 Peter 1:20 that applies to these brothers and sister as well as to us, and that says, "knowing this first, that no prophesy of Scripture is of any private interpretation, for prophesy never came by the will of man, but men of God spoke as they were moved by the Holy Spirit." There can be no doubt that every single moment has been, is, and will be planned by this all-knowing God of love.

BUT I HAVE CALLED YOU MINE

Thinking back to my day of Salvation, remembering that I was not looking for God, but was depressed and alone. I did not know what to do or what tomorrow would hold for my children me. In no way could God's plan have entered my mind because not being sure if He existed, how could He have helped me. Oh, how much I missed out on, but it was not too late, there was a great and powerful God who loved me and had a plan for me.

Having no idea that He knew me and wanted me to be His child, I kept walking in darkness. Never having read the Bible, there was no awareness of the thousands of promises this God had written to His believers. Only a punishing God was made known to me, so I was afraid of Him. However, after Salvation, the Bible told me of this loving and forgiving Savior, whose Father sent Him to die in my place.

The Scripture that impressed me the most was Romans 8:1 where it says, "There is therefore now no condemnation to those who are in Christ Jesus." One thing the Lady who had led me to the Lord had made sure I understood, was that I was now in Christ Jesus, and this was most on my mind. And the second one was Romans 8: 38 and 39 telling me that nothing and no one can separate me from the love of God which is in Christ Jesus my Lord.

From then on everything changed, having lost my car and therefore my job, my loving God gave me a job at Campus Crusade for Christ. Having been there now for 45 years and enjoyed every moment the Lord has used me to lead tens of thousands into His waiting arms. Since this special day, my children and I have not needed anything, and the rest of my family followed us into the kingdom of this merciful God.

So now, at the age of 85, my biggest joy is still working fulltime for Campus Crusade for Christ, which is now called CRU, and still have those private ministries with high school youth in different places. How could I ever thank my God enough for all the love and mercy He has shown, and I know that He will never stop this. By His grace, it will be my way of life forever and am allowed to tell other people about Him.

WHEN THERE IS A NEW SEASON, GO WITH IT

Having asked my Maker to let me continue to prove what is that good and acceptable and perfect will of His, as told in Romans 12:2, I will listen more than ever for His beloved voice. This voice has never led me astray and He will not start now, He promised that He is the same yesterday today and forever. He is so very dependable and says He never lies, so my future is secure, no fears or worries. I will continue to enjoy my journey because He has given me a good sense by now, to follow His leading.

My beloved Savior says in Proverbs 11:30 "The fruit of the righteous is a tree of life and he who wins souls if wise." Well, this is what my plan is more than ever and I will listen to the good advice of wisdom as she speaks in Proverbs 2:1 and 2, "My son if you receive my words and treasure my commands within you, so that you incline your ear to wisdom and apply your heart to understanding, if you cry out for discernment, and lift up your voice for understanding" and so beautifully continues in verse

5 "Then you will understand the fear of the Lord, and find the knowledge of God."

I learned so much from Proverbs and it was always the most important part of the Bible for my oldest son, he spent much of his time in Proverbs. It says in verse :7 "The fear of the Lord is the beginning of wisdom" and goes on in verse :8 and :9, " My son hear the instructions of your father and do not forsake the law of your mother, for they will be a graceful ornament on your head and chains about your neck." I will not fight what my Creator has chosen for me, because I know it will be the very best for me.

Loving what Ephesians 1:13 says so much, because sealing is so very final, it promises and confirms a permanent position. Even in government a seal is final, so it promises a claim for us saying "In Him you also trusted after you heard the word of truth, the Gospel of your Salvation, in Whom also, having believed, you were sealed with the Holy Spirit of promise, Who is the guarantee of our inheritance." I can hardly believe such an awesome promise, not only having been sealed, but this powerful Creator is even giving a guarantee for His promise.

NO TURNING BACK – NO TURNING BACK

This was the was the first Christian song my sons and I ever learned in our new church, and I still sing it now. There is no end to these awesome promises, that is why, after living and walking with this powerful loving God for 48 years, there is no turning back. This I can claim, having experienced the unbelievable faithfulness of my Creator.

It says so beautifully in Galatians 4:6 "and because you are sons, God has sent forth the Spirit of His Son into our hearts, crying out Abba, Father!" I know for a fact that Abba means Daddy, because in my 15 times of being in Israel, the children called their father Abba. These precious promises do not seem to end, they are so encouraging and uplifting. Memorizing some of them, helped brighten even the dark and lonely days.

Having experienced those dark and lonely days, before my Savior entered my life, this is a very sure and true statement. Of all those times when Satan tried his deceiving tactics on me, I could not say, excuse me, let me get my Bible. I had to have an answer ready right then, and it better had been a biblical answer because non other would have helped.

Well, that beautiful promise in Galatians continues in verse :7 as He promises, "Therefore you are no longer a slave but a son, and if a son then an heir of God through Christ." Being able to depend on these promises, I was no longer hovering in fear before my enemy, but was able to face his deceptions with a powerful assurance of the great God for ever in me.

NOW I CALL YOU FRIENDS

I t is in John 15:15 that my beloved Savior says, "No longer do I call you servants, for a servant does not know what his master is doing, but I have called you friends, for all things that I heard from my Father I have made known to you."

This is not all, even though this alone would make me want to follow Him but there is so much more to make me want to be close to Him. He tells me in verse :16 of John 15, " You did not choose Me, but I chose you and appointed you that you should go and bear fruit, and that your fruit should remain, that whatever you ask the Father in My name He may give you."

I can vouch not having chosen Him, but He chose me. It was a total surprise. My beloved Savior goes on in verse :20 "Remember the word that I said to you, a servant is not greater than his master. If they persecuted Me, they would also persecute you. If they kept My word, they would keep yours also." This is a powerful prayer that I will add to my list right now, because I really want Him to make me ready for persecution.

I love knowing that all the words He had me speak, are being kept by all who heard them. Yet another prayer of mine would be

Psalm 119:116 and:117, which say "Uphold me according to Your word, that I may live, and do not let me be ashamed of my hope. Hold me up, and I shall be safe, and I shall observe Your statutes continually."

Once again, the only way I will be able to observe His statutes is by being in His word as much as possible and pay close attention to His beloved voice. His holding me up will not happen if my mind is constantly in the world. Gratefully I acknowledge His reminding me of His presence when my mind has been in the world half of my day.

I KNEW YOU BEFORE I MADE THE WORLD.

One of my favorite Scripture to teach on was always Psalm 139 because it says so much about the future of the Youths I taught, which I wanted them to know. Especially how long their God had known them, and that He knew them before He even made the world. Using Ephesians 1:4 and 5 for this, remembering how totally surprised I was when learning that He knew me and chose me before He made the world. This would mean that He knew I was a sinner, yet He still wanted me.

Wow, I just could not believe this and read it again and again till it became real, and I was able to believe. When the enemy attacked, it was always a choice to run and hide or remember Who was my refuge and protection the last time. Especially in the past two years, with the world problems, the one thing that I ran to was Psalm 91. I encouraged my friends and family to do the same. Almost everything it says, applies to this worldwide pestilence, it was very comforting.

The first part applied to every believer because we dwell in the secret place of the Most High, so we shall abide under the shadow of the Almighty. Therefore, I will say of the Lord "He is my refuge and my fortress, my God, in Him I will trust." But then it continues so perfectly, "Surely, He shall deliver you from the snare of the fowler and from the perilous pestilence." It also says so adequately that you shall not be afraid of the pestilence that walks in darkness.

Now that I am 85, I especially learned that maturity is trusting in God, not in myself and growing in Him builds that trust. Moving away from self-took long, however, I finally got rid of those weeds of trusting in myself all the time. Jesus was asked in John 6:28 "what shall we do, that we may work the works of God?" Jesus answered and said to them, "This is the work of God, that you believe in Him whom He sent."

When they asked Jesus for bread Jesus said in verse :35, "I am the bread of life. He who comes to Me shall never hunger and he who believes in Me shall never thirst." Then this beloved Savior says in verse 39, "this is the will of Him who sent Me, that of all He has given Me I should lose nothing, but should raise it up at the last day." Jesus then repeats that promise in verse :40, "and this is the will of Him who sent Me, everyone who sees the son, and believes in Him may have everlasting life, and I will raise him up at the last day."

ARE THERE STILL TEMPTATIONS?

S ince the Father has scheduled me to become like His beloved Son, it would be pretty sure that He will not let me get away now, right? He has promised to never leave me or forsake me, right? So, I can depend on His presents with me as always, right? Wow, what brought on those doubts while I was taking a break for this Sunday, this has not happened in a while, I am truly surprised.

Holding still, like my Savior tells me so often, I try to sort out my feelings and find out my believe in my God has not changed. Spending a few hours with some Christian friends at a monthly luncheon and singing some spiritual songs got me back on track. It is amazing, perhaps I had been too long alone in my room writing on my book, needing some Christian fellowship.

One thing my Creator taught me early in my Christian life is not to talk too much because some of it was foolishness and waste. He really helped me with being still, and I could not believe how much more I heard and was aware of. This was because, when someone was talking to me, I was already busy figuring what my answer should be and so missed some of what was being said.

My Lord showed me Isaiah 50:4 which says, "The Lord has

given me the tongue of the learned, that I should know how to speak a word in season to him who is weary." So I immediately memorized that verse, and I listen better and talked less. Being quieter has benefits, it makes me more aware of what goes on around me, which is a benefit to be grateful for.

My beloved Father convinced me in Hebrews 5:14, that those who, by reason of use, have their senses exercised to discern both good and evil. He continues in 6:1, therefore, leaving the discussion of the elementary principles of Christ, let us go on to perfection.

To me that means to go on learning about and seeking that wise and all-knowing God, who promises us there is unending wisdom in His Word. It also means to daily put on that powerful armor of God which covers every part of our body. Having always liked when it calls the sword of the spirit the word of God.

NO OTHER GOSPEL

From the first day I heard that Word of God, for some reason it made total sense to me even though the why had not been explained to me yet. It was so amazing as that knowledge grew into a personal relationship with this awesome God. Through Campus Crusade it continued to grow into a love for reaching others who did not know Him yet. I never imagined to be writing books and it has been a joy to be able to re-live all these blessed times and adventures

It says so beautifully about increasing the knowledge of God in Hebrews 5:14 "But solid food belongs to those who are of full age, that is, those who by reason of use have their senses exercised to discern both good and evil." Reason of use, means to me continuously learning from the teachings of God's word and messages from His people. Having enjoyed many conferences both through church and Campus Crusade, made the fellowships so meaningful and some of them lasting.

Obeying my beloved God has become easy after experiencing all those blessings after each act of obedience. The strongest advice to me is in Deuteronomy 28, where eleven promises are announced ending in "so you shall not turn aside from any of the words which I command you this day, to the right or the left, to go after other gods to serve them." There are 14 blessings and 54 verses of coursings. Wow, I will do everything to stay in the blessings and not offend my merciful God.

I strongly feel that staying in my Father's blessing and live in His rest is to wait on his plans and directions. It is so beautifully expressed in Psalm 27:14 where it tells us, "Wait on the Lord, be of good courage, and He shall strengthen your heart, wait I say on the Lord." The thousands of promises my Savior wrote down for His children were to make this Christian life easy for them. What I have been most grateful for all these years has been the awareness of His presence at times of loss and danger.

Waiting seems to be very important to this loving God, it is mentioned so often, another time in Isaiah 30:18, "Therefore the Lord will wait, that He may be gracious to you, and therefore He will be exalted, that He may have mercy on you. For the Lord is a God of justice, blessed are all those who wait for Him." And my favorite is "Those who wait on the Lord shall renew their strength, they shall mount up with wings like eagles, they shall run and not be weary, they shall walk and not faint." At my age I review this one often.

ANOTHER CHANGE FOR MY LIFE

My director for the past two years has retired, and this particular department of the Jesus Film is being closed. This means I have to find another position, hopefully also in with the Jesus Film. I have been there for 40 of my 45 years with Campus Crusade and have totally enjoyed it. So as always, I will trust and wait on my beloved Father to place me just where I am needed since He knows what my talents are.

Worry is no longer in my vocabulary, this would be totally unfair to Him after all the guidance He has given me all these years. I have once again asked My beloved Savior to place me where He wants me and where I am most needed. Only He knows what my talents are, since He is the One who gave them to me.

There is truly no better way to live than in than in the presence of this almighty Creator, having the security of His presence and protection. It would not have been possible for me to handle the messed-up life I had, without the loving hand of this Savior. I will never again live without the instructions from His love letter.

Longing to be wise in my choices, I asked my Creator to make His will for me extra clear, so I do not miss anything He has for me. It is too late in my life to listen to my own wisdom, having seen the outcome of that. Wanting to know if it is His will for me to continue this writing after this book number six, one of the answer I understood was Habakkuk 2:2 " Than the Lord answered me and said, "Write the vision and make it plain on tablets, that he may run who reads it."

My Lord also says in Jeremiah 29:11, "For I know the thoughts that I think towards you Hannah, says the Lord, thoughts of peace and not of evil, to give you a future and a hope." Writing that scripture on everybody's cards, whatever they are for, gives me pleasure because it tells them that their God gives them a future and a hope. This has actually been the first time that I ever put my own name in there and I enjoyed that. It gives me great comfort to hear that my beloved Father thinks thoughts of peace toward me.

HAVING SEEN THE GOODNESS OF THE LORD

What a joy to listen to my Saviors encouraging advice, like in Psalm 27:13 and :14, were it expresses my thoughts when it says, "I would have lost heart, unless I had believed that I would see the goodness of the Lord in the land of the living." Having to admit that I have truly seen the goodness of the Lord in all my unbelievable adventures, I refuse to be afraid of the future.

I will always treasure my Saviors calling and the purpose He had for my life, and will trust Him with the rest that is left of it.

IN AMERICA FOR 63 YEARS

When I came to the US in 1959, the movie "Around the world in 80 days" had come out and I was just learning English. Watching this movie, I could test how good my English was, just as reading the Bible told me how well I knew God. Becoming a Christian in 1974, made me anxious to know this Creator who loved me, I listened to pastor's messages and attended Christian conferences.

Attending a good, Bible teaching church was vital for my two sons and I and we enjoyed every message taught. My two daughters were married and also grew in the Lord. These teachings were all wonderful news for us, and we had agreed for half an hour Bible study before the TV went on every evening. It was a great way to get my boys through their teen years and Proverbs told the truth about them not departing from it when they grew old.

One thing we liked beside teachings about Salvation, was Revelation and we talked often about it. We would discuss and choose where we would like to live or what we would do when we come back to earth in the millennium. My two boys and I even led a Mormon neighbor family to the Lord through these talks and into our church. We even stayed friends till the three kids were married and moved away.

It was a blessing how this awesome God led us into a greater knowledge of Himself and He became more real and a part of our lives as we aged. So, now my children and I go by what Titus says in 2:1 3 we are "looking for the blessed hope and glorious appearing of our great God and Savior Jesus Christ. We long for the Holy Spirit to fill this world with His presence so it will find peace.

We believers should truly ask the Holy Spirit to hover over the earth again as He did at the very beginning in Genesis 1:2 and see all that went wrong. Only He is the one who can give the desire to reach out in love for each other. I will ask for discernment for us believers learning how to solve the problem or to leave it totally to His wisdom and understanding.

NOT ASHAMED OF WITNESSING ANYMORE

The longer I harbor something negative in my heart, the bigger it gets. Forgiving and letting go of it is the best way, because that leaves the air free and clear for prayer. This way I can claim Ephesians 3:20, "Now to Him who is able to do exceedingly abundantly above all that we ask or think, according to the power that works in us, to Him be the glory."

It says that it is the Holy Spirit who is the power in me, so I learned to leave my situations in His hands. My first times of witnessing were embarrassing to me because I was afraid of what they think of me and would mock me. However, I was surprised that the listeners accepted what I had to share because it was given by the Holy Spirit.

Being ready to witness and talk about my faithful God began after I read Romans 1:16 which says, " For I am not ashamed of the Gospel of Christ, for it is the power of God to Salvation for everyone who believes, for the Jew first and also for the Greek."

As I began to fall more in love with my God, I enjoyed telling others about His love and His great qualifications. Feeling increasingly overwhelmed by Him, I enjoyed Psalms like 103:1-5, saying or singing "Bless the Lord oh my soul, and all that is within me, bless His holy name! Bless the Lord, oh my soul, and forget not all His benefits, Who forgives all your iniquities, Who heals all your diseases,

Who redeems your life from destruction, Who crowns you with lovingkindness and tender mercies, Who satisfies your mouth with good things, so that your youth is renewed like the eagle's." WOW, how would not every body want to love and follow a God like this. There are thousands of promises and encouragements like this in the love letter He wrote to His children.

GOD'S AWESOME FAITHFULNESS

Something else I love is Proverbs, which is packed with love professions and also warnings of what and who to stay away from. When my son Steve was in the Army, he spent almost all his free time reading and sharing the sayings of Proverbs. One of his cute stories is about his roommate with whom he was talking about the Bible.

Most of all I asked their heavenly Father to have Christian roommates for them, with whom they could study the Bible. Well, this precious God answered that prayer for both of them, and I will share their stories. Steve said that one night he and his roommate went to a military cafe, where young soldiers could go for fun. Steve's buddy had befriended a young lady whom he spent about two hours with.

This young lady got kind of affectionate and talked the young man into coming to her apartment with her. As they walked out, they told Steve about their departure and took off. Steve went outside, knowing that his roommate was his ride back to the base. Steve told me that he took a deep breath and sat down on the curve, asking the Lord to change his roommate's mind.

Suddenly, his roommate threw of the girl's arm, and walked back to Steve, telling him, "oh never mind, lets go home." Gratefully, my son sent a heartfelt thank you to His Savior and they both left for Base. How thankful this mother was for that report. It was such a blessing to know my Father is in control of my children's lives.

It was the same with my youngest son Bill. Because of his great love for the outdoors, especially trees, he had joined the California Conservation Corps. Besides fighting fires there was much landscaping to do, especially planting or removing trees. One of the days, the team had to remove an enormous old pine tree because of its space and discrepancy.

At one important job, my son's boss worked across from him, both using major equipment for this. Suddenly my son saw his directors name tag and said to him, you have the same last name as my sister. Bill's boss, lifted his head and looked at Bill's tag and said, you have the same last name as my sister-in-law. Laughing they discovered that they were brother-in-law's and a beautiful friendship developed.

This friendship became very close because they were not only physically, but more important spiritually related. David and his family were strong believers and made Bill a part of their family, took him to their church and have him at their home on the weekends. Once again, this faithful God answered my prayer as He did with Steve.

THE PEACE OF GOD WILL GUARD MY HEART AND MIND

P rayer has been always a very important part in my life and sometimes my heavenly Father answered even before I asked. There are so many verses in the Bible encouraging us to pray, I will mention only a few. For instance, in Colossians 4:2 "Continue earnestly in prayer, being vigilant in it with thanksgiving." It took me a long time before I liked praying, not until I realized hat it is just talking with my beloved Father.

The most popular verse about praying is in Philippians 4:6 and 7 "Be anxious for nothing but in everything by prayer and supplication, with thanksgiving, let your request be made known to God, and the peace of God, which surpasses all understanding, will guard your hearts and minds through Christ Jesus." I love that it says that the peace of God will guard my heart and mind, at my age I truly need that and even experienced it as well.

Praying for my family and friends everyday is special to me because it makes me feel like I have a part in their lives and there is no One greater I can bring them to. Another one like Romans

12:12 which says, "rejoicing in hope, patient in tribulation, continuing steadfastly in prayer." Our heavenly, merciful Father waits anxiously for us to have a loving conversation with His children to tell them of His deep care for them.

Another important subject our gracious Savior gave us in regard to prayer is in Matthew 6:6 saying "when you pray go into your room, and when you have shut your door, pray to your Father who is in the secret place, and your Father who sees in secret will reward you openly." Finding out that the prayer of a righteous man achieves much, helped me remember that I am righteous because I am in Christ Jesus and He is in me.

Realizing, what was not my Fathers plan for me, will not take place, this helped me to stop comparing myself with others. He has asked me to be faithful in what He needs me for. If I do not like or cannot handle what He desired for the current open door, He will just wait before He opens the next one. This does not mean my Lord is angry with me, it means I lose some of my Savior's blessings and He will choose someone else to do the job.

GOD'S WORD PRODUCES LIGHT AND GROWTH

My Savior gives such meaningful advice and encouragement about living this Christian life, its almost impossible to miss out. Even when failure happens, forgiveness is promised. As it tells in Colossians 2:6, "As you therefore have received Christ Jesus the Lord, so walk in Him, rooted and built up in Him and established in the faith, as you have been taught, abounding in it with thanksgiving.

Having truly experienced that light at times of loss, it saw me through grieve and disappointments and gave me great hope. It brought me that hope when my youngest son and his family moved to Kentucky and instead of seeing my grandchildren daily, it was now once a year. It also brought that light and hope when my oldest son and his wife moved to Wyoming, and I did not know when I would see them again. In both cases my loving God gave me His promised peace which passed my understanding.

My Lord's peace was also present at the death of my mother and sister, and even though grief was present, it was not like the grieve of unbelievers, who don't know that they will not see loved ones again. It was hurtful and lonely when my husband left our four children and me, knowing now how much the Lord's presence would have helped. Even though my perfection is not complete yet, my gratefulness for His guidance and encouragement is always strong as is that beautiful peace.

One thing showed me early in my Christian life is that there are consequences for disobedience, this happened in an incident with my two sons. We planned another of our loved picnics in the mountains, everything was arranged and packed up even the games. We laughed over some passed adventures and always thanked our heavenly Father for keeping us safe.

However, it was different this time and we would remember it for a while . When we arrived, we found a lovely spot near a water pool and a few very large boulders. Before the boys ran off to explore, I told them firmly not to climb that large boulder behind us. Explaining that it was totally worn smooth from the weather, therefore there was nothing to hold on to if they would slip.

OUR LORD IS STRONG ON OBEDIENCE FROM US

Making myself comfortable and getting my oil paints ready for a new painting, when I suddenly heard a loud yell behind me. Bill came running screaming that Steve had fallen off that large rock. Running as fast as possible I heard my son calling to me for help. Well, Steve had slipped off that smooth boulder and badly scraped his back on the dried-out bush he fell into. However, that was not the worst, he broke his leg.

Calling the paramedics, who assured me they would be right there, one of the campers gave them our location, and so we waited. After the drive to the hospital and the cast being put on Steve's leg, our afternoon fun was over but we thanked our Lord for His protection, even in this. Seeing Steve's sad face there was no need for me to say anything, however I made sure that our Bible study subject was on obedience that night.

There was no argument about it, the Lords words were very clear on that. Besides this, there were the missing out on his basketball games and the practices.

It was similar with my other son Bill, this young man loved climbing trees and we had many of those on our property. Having had a recent surgery on his head, I pleaded with him not to climb any trees till he was healed. Mentioning especially the front trees because they were his favorites and were lined along the cement sidewalk of our street. They were so dangerous for my son because there was very little room between the tree trunk and the cement.

I received a phone call at work around noon, from a Sheriff friend down the street, that Billy had fallen out of one of those front trees. Knowing about his head injury, this friend said his head hit the small area of grass, four inches away from the cement. Sending a heartfelt thank you to my God, I dashed off to see my injured son. What my friend did not want to tell me until I got there was that Billy had broken his right forearm and he offered to take us to the hospital.

Once again, as in Steve's case, Bill's absence from baseball was even more extended now than from his head injury. Hoping that the lessons from disobedience had truly kept on my son's mind, our beloved God had doubled the meaning of His instructions about being obedient. This wonderful, loving Creator never tires of showing His children mercy when they mess up and do not listen to instructions and wisdom. His love extends throughout their lives until they are safely with Him at home.

I AM STILL IN THE WORKS

Hear my beloved brethren, has not God chosen the poor of this world to be rich in faith and heirs of the kingdom, which He promised to those who love Him? The Lord's love letter is so full of wonderful promises that it is hard to be depressed, I love to have good music around me and think and read much about my awesome future. Also here is one of my most favorite scripture where my Savior promises in John 10:27-30

> "My sheep hear My voice, I know them, and they follow Me, and I give them eternal life, and they shall never perish, neither shall anyone snatch them out of My hand. My Father who has given them to Me is greater than all, and no one is able to snatch them out of My Father's hand. I and My Father are one."

Even after walking with my God for 48 years, I am still imperfect, yet to my Creator I am without spot or wrinkle according to Ephesian 5:27. This talks about His church: that He might present her to Himself a glorious church, not having spot or wrinkle or any such thing, but that she should be holy and without blemish. So, since I am part of His church, and His work is still being completed in me, that applies to me also, for which my heart is very grateful.

I must have a deeper relationship with my God if there is a true desire to help others, so my times with my Father and His beloved book cannot be neglected. My longing for His beautiful future plan can truly keep me from being afraid of it by my mind being much on this awesome Savior. He advises in Matthew 4:4 when Satan tempted Him, "man shall not live by bread alone, but by every word that proceeds from the mouth of God."

In my trips to those 27 countries my passport had to be always in order to be stamped with the right information. Otherwise, I would never have been able to get in or out of that country which was chosen this time. So, I must be ready for my final trip to my heavenly destination. If my entry papers are not stamped "forgiven and justified" I know my entry will be denied. That is why my merciful Savior speaks so much about being ready and prepared.

HONESTY IS VITAL TO GOD AND MY LIFE

It says in 2 Timothy 2:20 and :21, "But in a great house there are not only vessels of gold and silver, but also of wood and clay, some for honor and some for dishonor. Therefore, if anyone cleanses himself from the later, he will be a vessel for honor, sanctified and useful for the Master, prepared for every good work." I can only teach and show what is in my heart, otherwise I am a hypocrite always pretending.

It takes time learning to be real and honest in what and Who I am trying to portrait. I needed to stop pretending I am someone else or trying to be perfect. My energy must go into loving and helping others. In the days before my Salvation, I did not really know who I was or what I wanted or what my goal was for my life. Trying to be what others think can be totally frustrating and discouraging.

Especially if I felt that I was bad at something, I tried to cover it up or lied about it. Without this patient and loving God making me His child, it scares me to think where and what I would be today. All those good changes that came about in these past forty-eight years came because of the love this Creator has for me. He brought those changes about so gently without making me scared or run away.

This makes me so grateful for what my Savior was willing to do, which encourages me in Hebrews 2:14, "Inasmuch then as the children have partaken of flesh and blood, He Himself likewise shared in the same, that through death He might destroy him who had the power of death, that is the devil." It continues in verse :16, "For indeed He does not give aid to angels, but He does give aid to the seed of Abraham."

One of my favorite teachings to my precious youth continues with the above subject, saying in Ephesians 1:4, "just as the Father chose us in Jesus before the foundations of the world, that we should be holy and without blame before Him in love," continuing in :5, "having predestined us to adoption as sons by Jesus Christ to Himself, according to the good pleasure of His will," and in Verse:6, "to the praise of the glory of His grace, by which He made us accepted in the Beloved."

WOW, THIS IS AWESOME

These were such unbelievable promises, I have to take time out and read it over and over because it was so much, that I had trouble taking it all in. First of all, that He chose us before the foundation of the world means to me, that the Father and Son and Holy Spirit made this Salvation plan before the world was created.

They made that plan in love, and for us to be holy and blameless and accepted, they would have had to plan Jesus' death for our sins back then also. It's so amazing to me, every time I read and teach it, it truly shows that this awesome, triune God knew about our sins before They got into this mess, yet They went ahead with it anyway.

Only love could have done this, no other reason would have been big enough to go through so much pain and heartache. Thanks be to this God, that together they also planned the outcome of it, which is the greatest and most perfect blessing of all.

Being so grateful that the Creator said that what has been blessed cannot be cursed, this means that Satan has no power over me unless I give it to him. This leaves the choice once again to me and I try to pray every morning that my Lord will not allow me to fall into temptation but rather give me that way of escape.

The other request I try to remember daily is that I will not let His word ever slip away from my heart knowing that the enemy tries to steal it. I also think of His words being life and health and making the darkness flee from me. Praying His words over my family every day has shown to have results.

LORD YOU HEAR THE HUMBLE

My superiors say that it is important for me to share my work for the Lord with my supporters, so they know what their giving is being used for. The Bible tells me that I should be humble and not talk about the good things I am doing even though it is required by those who run this wonderful ministry. It says in Philippians 2:3, but in humility count others more significant than yourself

Humility means realizing that my ability and my confidence is given to me by God. It is written in 1 Peter 5:5 and 6,"Yes, all of you be submissive to one another, and be clothed with humility, for God resists the proud, but gives grace to the humble. Therefore, humble yourselves under the mighty hand of God, that He may exalt you in due time."

Being very cautious not to take any credit for my mission work, or my writing, I give the credit for it to my beloved Savior. Without His wisdom and input it would be impossible to keep Satan from his devilish interference. My pride would do more damage than good, and no compassion would be possible.

Since I would rather walk by faith and not by sight, I cannot believe anything that is being taught, it is vital that only the truth from His Word can enter my mind and heart. The enemies' lies must be carefully removed from what I believe.

It says so truthfully in 2 Corinthians 5:5 that God has prepared me for this very thing, and also has given me the Spirit as a guarantee for what is to come. He continues in verse :8 that I am confident, yes well pleased rather, to be absent from the body and to be present with the Lord. It closes in verse :9 whether present or absent, I long to be well pleasing to Him.

JUDGING IS DANGEROUS

Always having judged others so quickly and easily, this was something that had to be gone from my life. When I finally read this, it brought terror to my heart, because I would not like to be judged by my Savior. However, it took a long time to get rid of that habit of judging and begin to show mercy, as my Redeemer did.

Realizing that in order to judge someone, I had to think of myself being better than them. This is pride and I had come to hate pride because my God hates pride. Having come from dissatisfaction with myself, to being content with my life, and to being loved by my Creator, I was determent to fight any pride in me.

It is still not completed, and I still have to be sorry at times, but I realize each mistake quicker and reject it almost instant. This makes me grateful that my Father still works in me until that perfect body is mine forever. In the meantime, I will continue to serve Him and listen for that precious voice,

I can bring my Savior what I am, the good and the bad, the success and the failure and He will work it for good. He is able to take my failures and by His grace turn them into a blessing and make something helpful out of them. He keeps His promise to me of never leaving or forsaking me.

It is never too late to fall deeper in love with this awesome Creator and increase my service of leading others to Him. Making my God my everything, gets sweeter with time because it increases my commitment to Him. It also keeps showing me that my God never gets tired of refreshing and increasing our relationship.

SITTING AT HIS FEET

This continuous interest encourages me to stay close and faithful to Him, learning it from my Savior. Sitting at His feet and listening to, or reading those wonderful words has become a rewarding habit which I hope never to neglect. That is also what I fervently teach these precious youths He has entrusted to me.

The lessons I prepare for my students have been fed me by the Holy Spirit the same way He is feeding me the encouraging subjects for these books. They have been what has been given to me by Him, for which I am so grateful. Only He knows the subjects these precious brothers and sisters of mine want to hear.

Only this awesome Comforter knows the questions and problems His children have and with His wise examples influences my heart to share. From the raising of my children to the mission trips all over the world to now, sharing it all, has been His idea not mine from the very beginning. I am so grateful that I was obedient.

I hope He lets me continue, because as my legs can be less active, I still have a purpose by teaching and writing, so I am not useless yet. Even the work at the "Pregnancy Center" is much easier now, because the clients can get what they need for their babies once a month themselves and we only mark it down on their files.

Before we always had to go all the way back and forth to the storage till the clients had exactly what they needed, in the right size, color and style. It was much walking for us before, but our Father gave someone a much better idea and we are so grateful because it is so much easier on us.

THERE ARE ALWAYS IMPROVEMENTS

In all my times of growing and learning by trials, I ended up closer to the Lord, and therefore having less fear of hard times. Learning from Luke 2:52 that even Jesus increased in wisdom and stature, and in favor with God and men, so must I. Realizing that here is no standing still, because that would mean falling back.

It is the same with everything in life, I cannot just stop increasing and let life pass by me. It is vital that heart and soul are firmly grounded in my Savior in order for good things to come out of me. and to be useful to the One who called me into His service.

When my Creator made me His, there was no knowledge and wisdom in me yet. This only came by the times I spent in His presence and increasing my days and hours in His blessed word. How else could I have lived in His joy and peace without these awesome promises He wrote to His children.

My Father said so clearly in 2 Peter 3:9 that the Lord is not slack concerning His promise, but is longsuffering toward us, not willing that any should perish but that all should come to repentance. This shows the great love and patience this merciful God has, and that He never gives up on His believers.

The Creator said in Ephesians 1:4 and :5, that He knew me and chose me in Jesus before the foundation of the world. Then He waited another 37 years after my birth, before I was finally in His loving arms. Wow, that is what I truly call patience, I am far from this beautiful and everlasting talent.

PUT ON THE WHOLE ARMOR OF GOD

This is another of my favorite teachings but also the precious verse :8 first says, "knowing that whatever good anyone does, he will receive the same from the Lord." It is such a joy to pass on all these blessed promises. This goes on with the armor of God meaningful advice of putting that whole armor on every morning to help me through the day.

It so beautifully explains the different parts of the body being protected. It tells us in verse:11 that this is how we can stand against the wiles of the devil. And in :12, we do not wrestle against flesh and blood, but the rulers of the darkness of this age, against spiritual hosts of wickedness in the heavenly places.

It keeps on in :13, therefore, take up the whole armor of God, that you may be able to withstand in the evil day, and having done all, to stand. It tells me in verse :14 stand therefore, having girded your waist with truth, having put on the breastplate of righteousness.

Then, in verse :15, and having shod your feet with the preparation of the Gospel of peace, and in :16 above all, taking the shield of faith with which you will be able to quench all the fiery darts of the wicked one. And in :17, and take the helmet of Salvation, and the sword of the Spirit, which is the word of God.

These are such powerful instructions and wisdom that I Have to read it often to keep them on my mind and live by it all. It makes so much sense how the girdle, the heart, the waist, and the feet need protection to function correctly in the service of our beloved and merciful God.

ONE OF THE MOST POWERFUL THINGS JESUS PROMISED

I challenge you and want to share once more one of my favorite verses, Luke 10:19 and 20, "Behold I give you the authority to trample on serpents and scorpions and over **all** the power of the enemy, and nothing shall by any means hurt you. Nevertheless, do not rejoice that the spirits are subject to you, but that your names are written in heaven."

I love this so much because it finally gave me the courage to not be afraid so easily of everything that goes boo in the night. Being raised with such superstitious people, there was something scary behind every dark and unusual place and situation. But now I belong to a powerful and mighty God who promises me protection.

"Nothing shall by any means hurt you" that means so much to me because I am not such a scaredy-cat anymore. Hebrews 5:14 tells me that "solid food belongs to those who are of full age, that is, those who by reason of use have their senses exercised to be aware of both good and evil.

This makes me feel so secure because the one thing I have done right from the beginning is being daily in that precious powerful and life changing word of my God. There is every subject covered in my Creator's book of instructions, guidance and a strong conformation of His unconditional love.

Being so grateful not only that my Savior has taught me all these wonderful things that changed my live for the better, but the gentle and firm way He has done this. Always realizing that something good came out of it helped me to endure the chastening and wait to see what He had in mind this time.

GOD NEVER TEMPTS ANYONE

It is a great relieve that the Bible tells us in James 1:13 &:14, " let no one say when he is tempted, 'I am tempted by God' for God cannot be tempted by evil, nor does He Himself tempt anyone. But each of us is tempted when he is drawn away by his own desires and is enticed." My gratefulness is to my loving Savior who has paid for and given me all that is needed to live this Christian life, I just have to be willing to take the advice.

I used to spend way too much time letting the enemy keep me in guilt over mistakes that had been washed away by the blood of my Savior. The plan this powerful Creator came up with is so perfect, nothing has or will ever be changed about it, and I will forever praise Him about that.

My beloved God had brought me too far to let me go now and I have learned too much to turn away from Him. One of the first commitments my kids and I made is to follow Jesus, and never turn back. After all these years, this is more on our mind than ever, having learned the great faithfulness of our God.

Hoping with all my heart that this is the biggest lesson I have left in those I have taught, I will always pray that there was no turning back for them. It reminds me in Hebrews 11:6 that "without faith it is impossible to please God, for he who comes to God must believe that He is, and that He is a rewarder of those who diligently seek Him."

Jesus was in everything I have done and everywhere I went, if He had not been the center of my life, nothing would have been a success. The Lord still uses this child of His and brings new wine out of it. I will continue to write until my beloved God says "done". After these blessed and informative forty-eight years of being taught by this awesome God of love, I long to pass this on to anyone who will listen.

1 Corinthians 16:13 and 14 says "watch, stand fast in the faith, be brave, be strong. Let all that you do be done with love." This is my prayer for you and for me!!!

Printed in the United States
by Baker & Taylor Publisher Services